SPOTLIGHT ON PHYSICAL SCIENCE

CHEMICAL REACTIONS
IT MATTERS

RACHAEL MORLOCK

PowerKiDS press™
NEW YORK

Published in 2020 by The Rosen Publishing Group, Inc.
29 East 21st Street, New York, NY 10010

Copyright © 2020 by The Rosen Publishing Group, Inc.

All rights reserved. No part of this book may be reproduced in any form without permission in writing from the publisher, except by a reviewer.

Editor: Jennifer Lombardo
Book Design: Michael Flynn

Photo Credits: Cover, p. 1 jarabee123/Shutterstock.com; (series molecular background) pro500/Shutterstock.com; p. 5 (main)Dmitry Galaganov/Shutterstock.com; p. 5 (inset) Chones/Shutterstock.com; p. 6 Live and Learn/Shutterstock.com; p. 7 Monkey Business Images/Shutterstock.com; p. 9 (main) Bettmann/Getty Images; p. 9 (inset) Alex Andrei/Shutterstock.com; p. 11 (periodic table) Alejo Miranda/Shutterstock.com; p. 11 (atom) Designua/Shutterstock.com; p. 12 Ezume Images/Shutterstock.com; p. 13 Everett Historical/Shutterstock.com; p. 15 Double Brain/Shutterstock.com; p. 16 Andraž Cerar/Shutterstock.com; p. 17 VasiliyBudarin/Shutterstock.com; p. 18 vincent noel/Shutterstock.com; p. 19 Universal History Archive/Universal Images Group/Getty Images; p. 21 Andia/Universal Images Group/Getty Images; p. 22 Sabelskaya/Shutterstock.com; p. 23 Elena Schweitzer/Shutterstock.com; p. 24 Tom Wang/Shutterstock.com; p. 25 Bettmann/Getty Images; p. 27 (main) Kondratuk Aleksei/Shutterstock.com; p. 27 (inset) anko70/Shutterstock.com; p. 29 ullstein bild Dtl./ullstein bild/Getty Images.

Library of Congress Cataloging-in-Publication Data

Names: Morlock, Rachael, author.
Title: Chemical reactions : it matters / Rachael Morlock.
Description: New York : PowerKids Press, [2020] | Series: Spotlight on
  physical science | Includes index.
Identifiers: LCCN 2019017305| ISBN 9781725312944 (pbk.) | ISBN 9781725312975
  (library bound) | ISBN 9781725312951 (6 pack)
Subjects: LCSH: Chemistry--Juvenile literature.
Classification: LCC QD35 .M67 2020 | DDC 541/.39--dc23
LC record available at https://lccn.loc.gov/2019017305

Manufactured in the United States of America

CPSIA Compliance Information: Batch #CWPK20. For further information contact Rosen Publishing, New York, New York at 1-800-237-9932.

CONTENTS

THE SCIENCE OF CHANGE 4
IDENTIFYING CHEMICAL REACTIONS. 6
ELEMENTS MATTER 8
THE BUILDING BLOCKS: ATOMS 10
DALTON'S ATOMIC THEORY 12
CHEMICAL BONDS 14
COMBINE, BREAK, OR SWAP 18
IMPORTANT ENERGY 20
THE HEAT IS ON 22
EXPLOSIVE CHEMISTRY 24
NATURAL REACTIONS. 26
MASTERING REACTIONS 28
RECOGNIZING REACTIONS 30
GLOSSARY 31
INDEX 32
PRIMARY SOURCE LIST 32
WEBSITES. 32

CHAPTER ONE

THE SCIENCE OF CHANGE

Chemical reactions are constantly happening within your body and in the world around you. They can happen on their own, or they can be planned. Scientists and engineers use chemical reactions as tools to create and improve **technology** and power our lives. You probably use chemical reactions without realizing it! If you've ever toasted a slice of bread, then you've used a chemical reaction.

A chemical reaction is a process that creates a chemical change. When two or more substances come into contact with each other, a chemical reaction may take place. These substances are called reactants. If reactants come together and there's enough energy, they can produce something new and different. The new substance is called a product. Sometimes, a chemical reaction creates more than one product. Products can look, feel, and act very differently than the reactants that created them.

When you put bread in a toaster, heat energy changes the makeup of the bread. This chemical reaction creates toast, a new substance that has a darker color and harder **texture**.

5

CHAPTER TWO

IDENTIFYING CHEMICAL REACTIONS

Not all changes are chemical reactions. Scientists can tell if something is a chemical reaction by looking for certain signs. If the change can't be undone, that's one sign that a chemical reaction has occurred.

Since chemical reactions create new substances, finding a new material is another helpful clue. This material may take the form of a solid, liquid, or gas. Bubbles in a solution might mean that a new gas has been produced. Changes in color and texture can also point to a chemical reaction.

In this chemical reaction, soap and chemicals interact to produce a foamy substance known as elephant's toothpaste. The new material is a sign that a chemical reaction has taken place.

All chemical reactions require energy. If something gives off or takes in energy, that's another clue. Heat, light, sound, and electricity are different forms of energy. A chemical reaction might make a loud bang, cause a burst of fire, or let off a warm glow. These are all signs that energy is involved in the reaction.

CHAPTER THREE

ELEMENTS MATTER

The substances in a chemical reaction are made up of matter. Look around you. Everything you see is made of matter! Anything that takes up space and has mass is called matter. Anything that can be weighed has mass.

All matter is made up of elements. There are more than 100 elements, each with its own unique, or one-of-a-kind, properties. They come together in different combinations to make every single part of the universe.

Scientists began to understand how elements worked in the 1600s. In 1869, a scientist named Dmitri Mendeleev organized more than 200 years of discoveries into the periodic table of elements. Scientists have added to it since then. This tool gives a symbol for each element and information about what they are and how they work. Elements in the table are grouped together into families of similar elements.

Marie Curie, pictured here in her laboratory, was a scientist whose work added the elements polonium and radium to the periodic table. Her research earned her the 1911 Nobel Prize for **chemistry**.

84	88
Po	**Ra**
Polonium	Radium
[208.9824]	226.0254

CHAPTER FOUR

THE BUILDING BLOCKS: ATOMS

The universe is made of matter, matter is made of elements, and elements are made of atoms. Atoms are the basic building blocks of everything! An atom is the smallest part of an element that still acts like the element. All the atoms in one element are **identical** to each other.

Atoms are too small to see without special tools called microscopes, and they're made of even smaller parts. The tiny, thick center of an atom is called the nucleus. Particles called protons and neutrons are inside the nucleus. Protons have a positive charge, and neutrons are **neutral**. Together, they make the nucleus positive. An element's atomic number in the periodic table represents the number of protons it has. Particles called electrons move in a kind of cloud around the nucleus. Electrons have a **negative** charge that draws them to the positive nucleus.

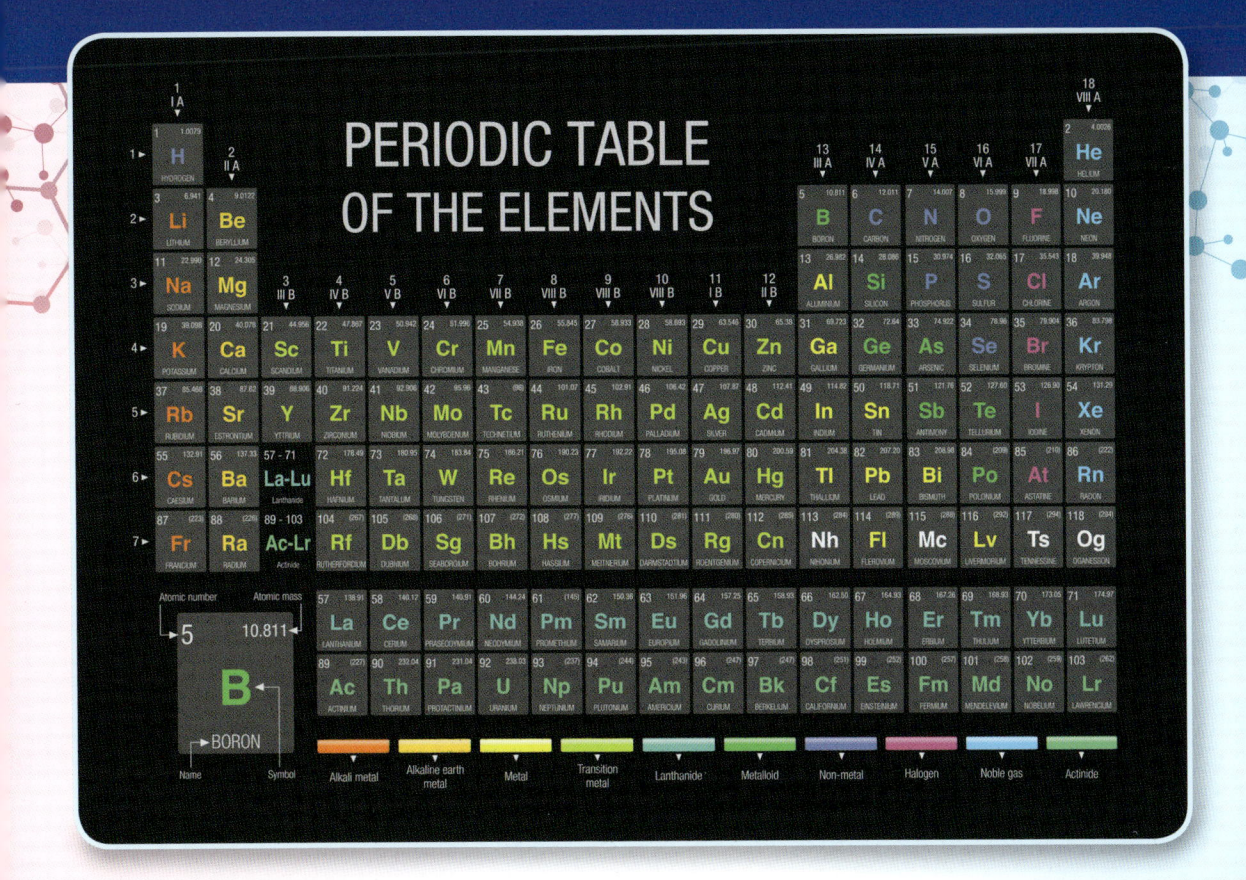

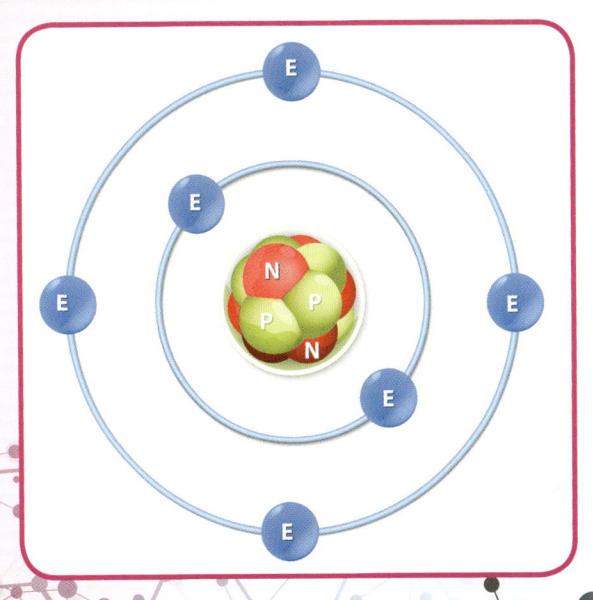

This model provides one way of looking at a carbon atom. Carbon's atomic number tells you that there are six protons in its nucleus. In this atom, six electrons travel around the nucleus.

CHAPTER FIVE

DALTON'S ATOMIC THEORY

By studying atoms, scientists have noticed patterns in the way they act. John Dalton was an English chemist who studied atoms in the 1800s. His observations helped him develop a **theory** to explain the rules that atoms follow. The first rule says that all matter is made up of atoms. The second rule explains that all the atoms of one kind of element are the same.

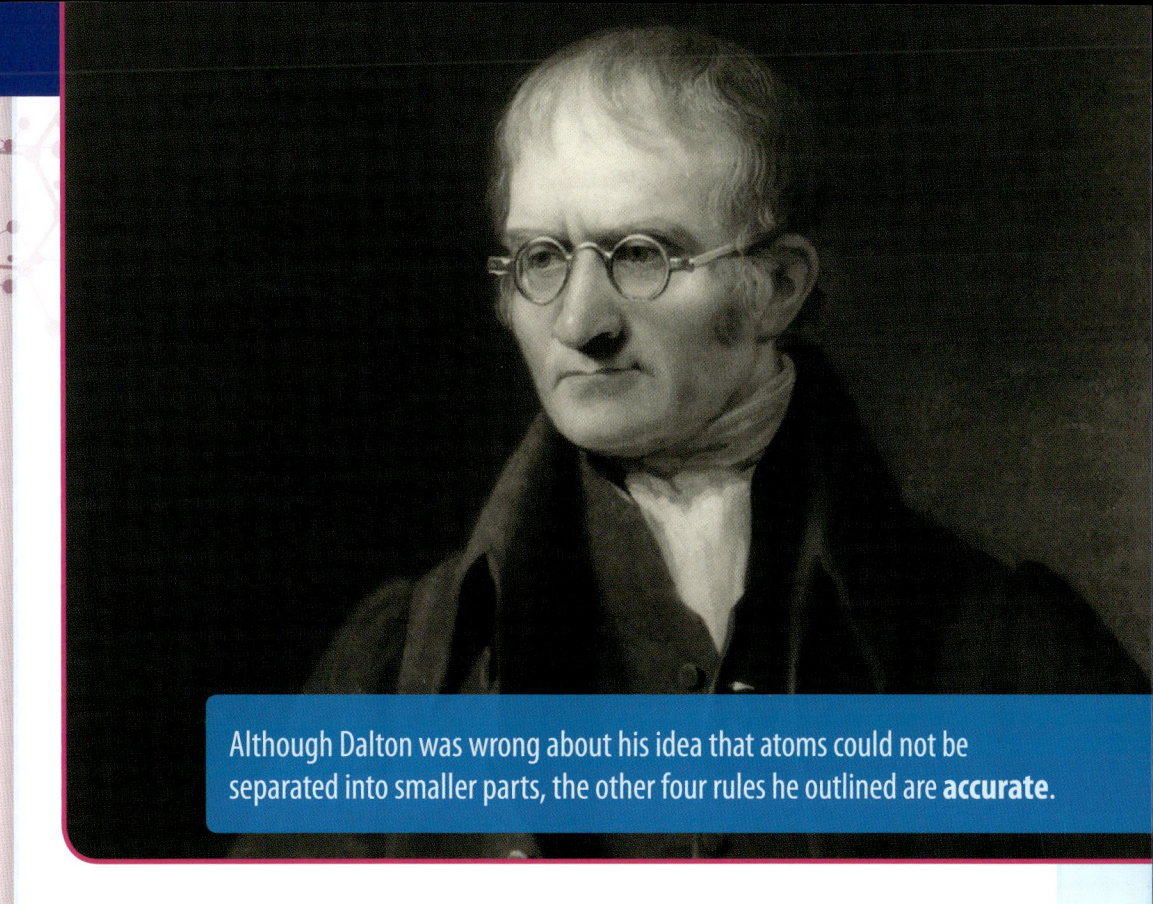

Although Dalton was wrong about his idea that atoms could not be separated into smaller parts, the other four rules he outlined are **accurate**.

The next two rules in Dalton's atomic theory are important for understanding chemical reactions. The third rule states that atoms can combine to make compounds. A compound is formed when atoms from different elements join together. For example, water is a compound of two different elements that bond together—hydrogen and oxygen. Dalton's fourth rule states that the bonds between atoms can change in a chemical reaction. Moving atoms around, or rearranging them, leads to new compounds and substances.

CHAPTER SIX

CHEMICAL BONDS

When atoms are rearranged in a chemical reaction, their chemical bonds change. Chemical bonds form through the activity of electrons. Although the number of protons and neutrons stays the same, a chemical reaction can change the number of electrons an atom has. Atoms from different elements can take, give, or share electrons. When they do, they form chemical bonds. The atoms can join together or break apart into new compounds.

Atoms that give or take electrons form ionic bonds. These bonds often connect a metal and a nonmetal element. Atoms that share electrons have covalent bonds. These bonds usually happen between two or more nonmetal elements. H_2O, or water, is formed by a covalent bond of the elements hydrogen and oxygen. In one molecule of H_2O, one oxygen atom shares electrons with two hydrogen atoms.

This **diagram** shows H_2O as both a compound and a molecule. A molecule is the smallest unit of a compound. It's a group of two or more atoms bonded together.

WATER – H$_2$O

OXYGEN

O

HYDROGEN

H

HYDROGEN

H

Scientists use chemical **equations** as a way to show in writing how chemical bonds form. For example, the salt people use on their food is formed by a chemical bond between the elements sodium (Na) and chlorine (Cl). Written as a chemical equation, it looks like this: $2\ NA + Cl_2 \rightarrow 2\ NaCl$. The sodium and chlorine are separate elements. They are the reactants. The arrow shows that a chemical reaction is taking place so the elements bond together to form a product. The new compound is called sodium chloride, or salt.

Sodium is an unstable metal. Chlorine is a dangerous gas. When they share electrons, though, they change into tasty crystals of salt. Even though the elements are the same, their atoms have been rearranged to form a chemically bonded compound. Because of the chemical bond, the product looks, feels, and acts very different from the reactants.

SODIUM

On its own, sodium is a dangerous metal that can easily burst into flames. It can be transformed by a chemical reaction into part of a safe compound.

CHAPTER SEVEN

COMBINE, BREAK, OR SWAP

Scientists pay attention to the way chemical reactions happen. They divide chemical reactions into types based on the patterns they follow. The types of chemical reactions include combination, decomposition, and displacement reactions.

Some reactions happen when two or more elements, molecules, or compounds combine. These are called combination reactions, and they form only one product. The opposite of combination is decomposition. In a decomposition reaction, one compound breaks apart and forms two or more products.

Hydrogen peroxide is a chemical compound made of oxygen and hydrogen. It's stored in a dark bottle. That's because light can cause a decomposition reaction that breaks the compound apart into water and oxygen.

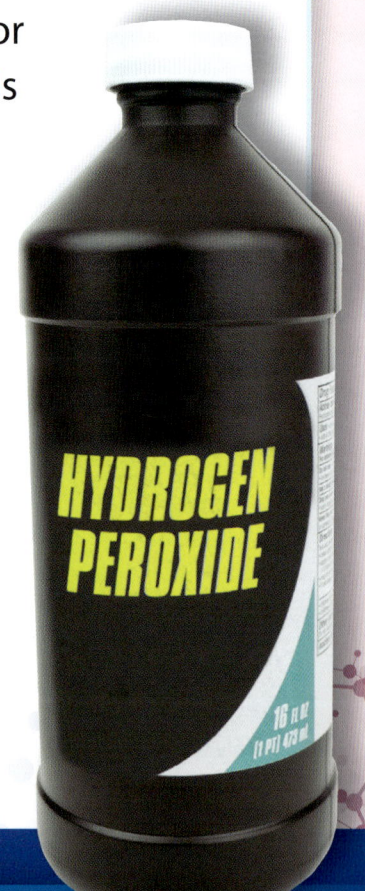

Someone who studies chemistry is called a chemist. Shown here is French chemist Louis Jacques Thénard, who lived from 1777 to 1857.

    Instead of coming together into one product or breaking apart into a few, sometimes elements simply switch places. This is called a displacement reaction. In single displacement, one element and one compound come together. The element takes the place of another element in the compound, leaving the other element on its own. In double displacement, the elements from two different compounds swap places.

CHAPTER EIGHT

IMPORTANT ENERGY

Energy plays an important role in the way atoms give, take, or share their electrons to form chemical bonds. Remember that an atom's electrons are attracted to the positive charge of its nucleus. Energy is needed for electrons to break away from that charge or form bonds with other atoms.

Every chemical reaction is an interaction between matter and energy. For this to happen, atoms need to make contact by **colliding** into each other, so there must be enough energy to make the atoms start moving.

The energy that starts a chemical reaction often takes the form of light, heat, or electricity. The amount of energy available can change the speed of a reaction. By adding energy, you can start or speed up a reaction. Taking it away can slow down or stop a reaction.

Shown here is a scientist experimenting with catalysts. A catalyst is a substance that can be added to start or speed up the rate of a reaction.

21

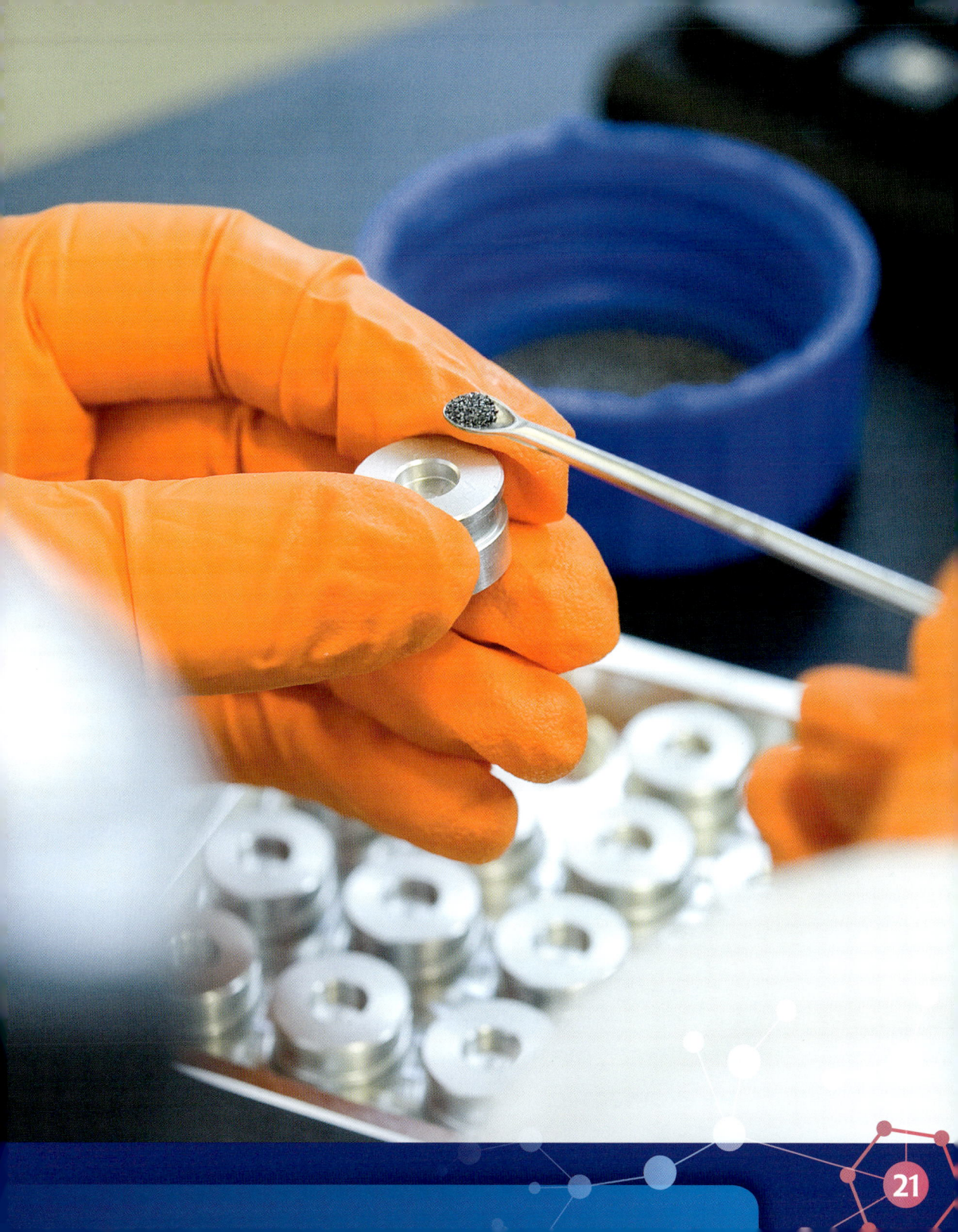

CHAPTER NINE

THE HEAT IS ON

Many chemical reactions involve energy in the form of heat. How heat is involved depends on whether chemical bonds are broken or built. Heat is absorbed when bonds are broken. It is released when bonds are built.

Breaking bonds takes a lot of energy, so the reaction absorbs energy in the form of heat from the surrounding area. This is called an endothermic reaction. A first aid cold pack, which has chemicals in it instead of ice, is an example of something that uses an endothermic reaction. When the chemicals in the pack mix together, they use up heat from their surroundings. As a result, the pack gets cold.

Reactions that build bonds and release heat are called exothermic. Building bonds takes less energy than breaking them. Exothermic reactions give off extra energy as heat and warm up their surroundings. Any **combustion** reaction, such as that in a firework, is exothermic. In fact, most reactions are exothermic.

Reactions that involve fire, such as lighting a candle, are exothermic. The fire gives off energy in the form of light and heat.

23

CHAPTER TEN

EXPLOSIVE CHEMISTRY

Combustion is a type of chemical reaction that's responsible for exciting firework displays and comforting campfires. It's also responsible for explosions. Combustion creates heat, light, and fire. It provides powerful examples of chemical reactions in action.

On May 6, 1937, an airship filled with hydrogen caught fire over New Jersey. The *Hindenburg* used this lighter-than-air gas to fly. Unfortunately, the gas is also very **flammable.**

Oxygen usually makes combustion possible. When oxygen combines with some compounds, it releases energy in the form of heat, along with carbon dioxide and water vapor. Sometimes, combustion also creates unwanted products such as soot, **pollutants**, and dangerous fumes. If the oxygen is removed from the reaction, combustion and burning will stop.

Combustion is a type of oxidation-reduction, or redox, reaction. These involve oxygen. In many redox reactions, oxygen is lost by one compound and gained by another. Another example of a redox reaction is the way the insides of some fruits, such as apples and bananas, turn brown when they're exposed to oxygen in the air.

CHAPTER ELEVEN

NATURAL REACTIONS

Chemical reactions are constantly happening inside your body and in nature. When you take a deep breath, your body uses oxygen in a chemical reaction. Animals use this chemical reaction called respiration to provide the energy they need to live. Inside your cells, **glucose** and oxygen react to produce carbon dioxide, water, and energy.

Green plants reverse this chemical reaction in a process called photosynthesis. With energy from sunlight, carbon dioxide and water react to produce glucose and oxygen. Plants use glucose as fuel and return oxygen into the atmosphere. That's the same oxygen we use in respiration!

Many other natural processes happen through chemical reactions. Our bodies digest food and grow through chemical reactions. Fossils form as chemical reactions break down once-living things. Weathering changes the sides of mountains in chemical reactions that take place over millions of years.

FIREFLY

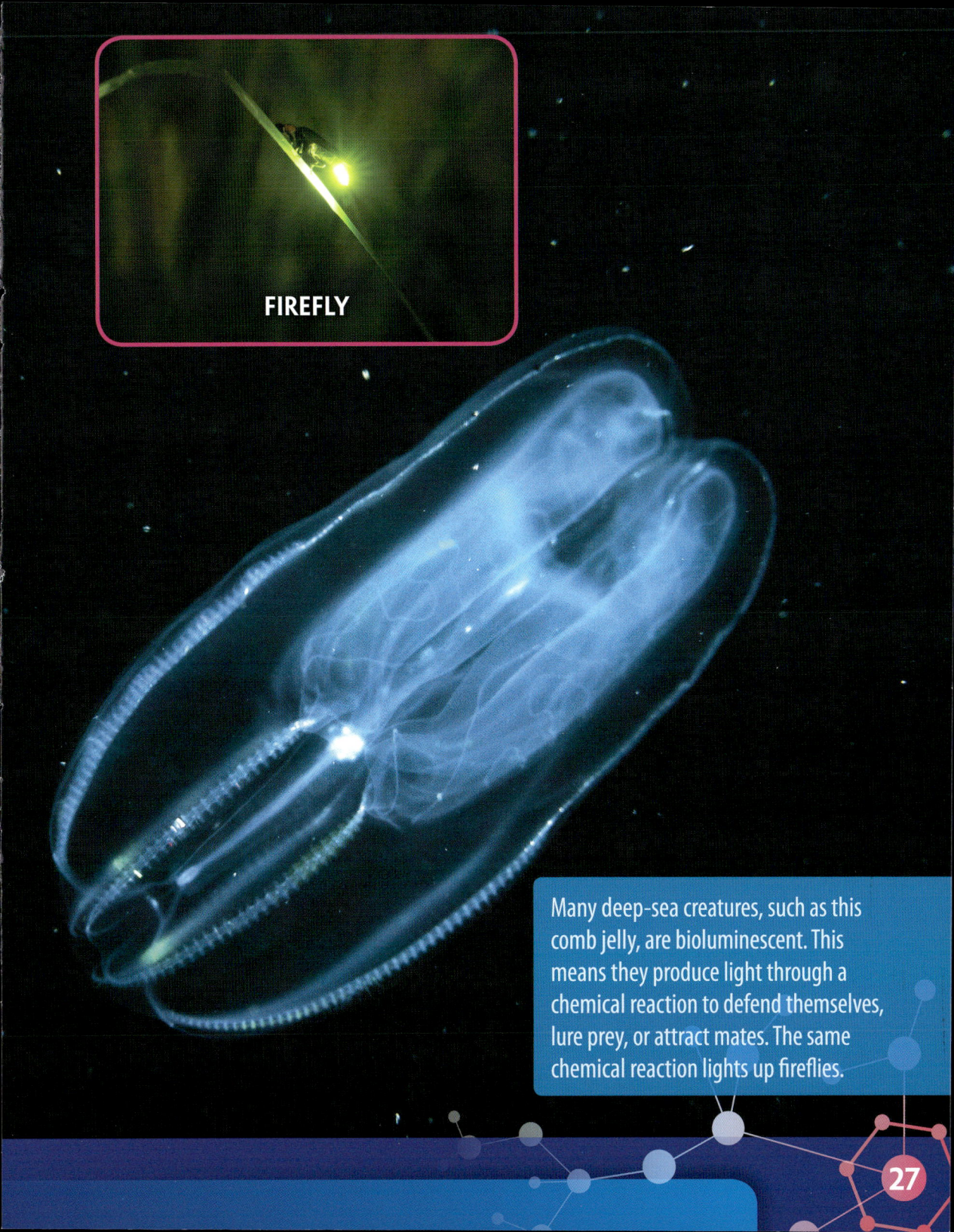

Many deep-sea creatures, such as this comb jelly, are bioluminescent. This means they produce light through a chemical reaction to defend themselves, lure prey, or attract mates. The same chemical reaction lights up fireflies.

27

CHAPTER TWELVE

MASTERING REACTIONS

Humans have found ways of using chemical reactions as tools. Cooking is one of the everyday chemical reactions people use to make life better. Others include burning gasoline to power a car, taking medicine to treat a disease, or using a battery to power a flashlight.

One of the most important chemical reaction breakthroughs happened in 1909. Scientists Fritz Haber and Carl Bosch created a new way of making fertilizer. For the first time, people could take nitrogen and hydrogen from the air and use this process to produce a compound called ammonia. Ammonia can be used to make fertilizer that helps plants and crops grow. This human-made fertilizer made it possible to grow more food and feed more people than ever before in human history.

The Haber-Bosch process was an important historical event. Shown here is a factory where workers used this chemical process to make fertilizer.

29

CHAPTER THIRTEEN

RECOGNIZING REACTIONS

Life couldn't exist without chemical reactions! Everything you see and use in life is the result of matter such as elements coming together and producing new substances. This often happens naturally, but sometimes people bring elements together to produce something beautiful, useful, or life-changing. Today, scientists and engineers are constantly at work finding new ways that chemical reactions can advance technology.

Whether you're enjoying the human-made colorful blasts of fireworks on a summer night or watching the natural flashing lights of a firefly, chemical reactions shape and color the universe. The next time you take a deep breath, bake a cake, or light a candle, think about the ways chemical reactions are at play around and within you. The transformation of one substance into another may look like magic, but it's just another example of science at work in the world.

GLOSSARY

accurate (AA-kyuh-ruht) Free of mistakes.

chemistry (KEH-muh-stree) A science that deals with substances, their properties, and the changes they go through.

collide (kuh-LYD) To come together with a big impact.

combustion (kuhm-BUHS-chuhn) The act of burning.

diagram (DYE-uh-gram) A drawing that explains or shows the parts of something or how something works.

equation (ih-KWAY-zhuhn) A statement that two expressions are equal.

flammable (FLA-muh-buhl) Easily set on fire.

glucose (GLOO-kohs) A naturally occurring sugar.

identical (eye-DEN-tih-kuhl) Alike in every way.

negative (NEH-guh-tiv) Having more electrons than protons.

neutral (NOO-truhl) Without an electrical charge.

pollutant (puh-LOO-tuhnt) Something that makes air, water, or soil dirty.

technology (tehk-NAH-luh-jee) The way people do something and the tools they use.

texture (TEKS-chuhr) The way something feels to the touch.

theory (THEE-uh-ree) An idea or set of ideas intended to explain something.

INDEX

A
atoms, 10, 11, 12, 13, 14, 16, 20

B
bonds, 13, 14, 16, 20, 22

C
catalysts, 20
combination reaction, 18
combustion, 22, 24, 25
compounds, 13, 14, 16, 17, 18, 19, 25, 28
covalent bonds, 14

D
decomposition reaction, 18
displacement reaction, 18, 19

E
electricity, 7, 20
electrons, 10, 11, 14, 16, 20
elements, 8, 10, 12, 13, 14, 16, 18, 19, 30
endothermic reaction, 22
energy, 4, 5, 7, 20, 22, 25, 26
exothermic reaction, 22, 23

F
fire, 7, 23, 24, 25

H
heat, 5, 7, 20, 22, 23, 24, 25

I
ionic bonds, 14

L
light, 7, 20, 23, 24

M
matter, 8, 10, 12, 20, 30
molecule, 14, 18

N
neutrons, 10, 14
nucleus, 10, 11, 20

O
oxidation-reduction (redox) reaction, 25

P
periodic table, 8, 10, 11
products, 4, 16, 18, 19
protons, 10, 11, 14

R
reactants, 4, 16

PRIMARY SOURCE LIST

Page 9
Scientist Marie Curie (Maria Sklodowska) in her laboratory. Photograph. Circa 1890. Bettmann.

Page 13
John Dalton. Illustration. c. 1895. Shutterstock.

Page 25
Crew members fleeing from burning *Hindenburg* airship. Photograph. May 6, 1937. Bettmann.

WEBSITES

Due to the changing nature of Internet links, PowerKids Press has developed an online list of websites related to the subject of this book. This site is updated regularly. Please use this link to access the list: www.powerkidslinks.com/sops/chemreact

Chemical reactions : it matters